Copywriting Gems
For A Small Business Owner

Most business owners are not aware of the treasure within their reach. The treasure has a name. It's called Copywriting.

This small book reveals certain aspects of the magic of copywriting, having a small business owner in mind.

The lessons are IMMEDIATELY actionable and can transform the way you see and conduct your business.

What does copywriting mean to your business?

It means more leads, more sales, taking and conducting business online. It could transform your business and your life.

Vlad Tseytkin

TABLE OF CONTENTS

How An Innocent 10-Minute Chit Chat On The Beach In Miami Turned Into A Transformational Business Breakthrough.
A Miracle Of A COPY OF SUCCESS.

"This is so frustrating. I know, success is a blessing, but can you call this life a blessing?"

I wasn't sure how to react, as it seemed as a blessing to me. It was the beginning of January. A warm and beautiful day in Miami. Soft breeze cooling the raging sun.

The pain and frustration Dave felt on the last day of his vacation didn't harmonize well with the surrounding calm and beauty.

Dave was very successful. Advertising on TV, radio, newspapers brought him clients. There was a 3-step process in place. Advertising -> a short phone consultation -> an hour long office consultation. At the end of an office consult 9 out of 10 people bought products and services. 9 out of 10!

So what was the cause of the frustration?

Throughout the years, he hired many people. He trained them to do what he was doing. He trained them well -

taught, explained, demonstrated.

No matter how much he tried, no matter how much he paid, nobody was able to achieve the same results. His 9 out of 10 against anybody else's 1-2 out of 10.

He had staff. The staff was good. They did all the paperwork and technical work. Dave himself had to do the key activities - otherwise his business would die. It was him, personally, who must do both, phone consultations, and office consultations. Day in, day out.

Day off? Vacation? Sick in bed? Family trip?

Lost prospects, angry clients, zero revenue.

The sun was about to set, touching the edge of the ocean. I said, "Dave, I'm about to tell you something. But I don't want to waste time explaining or proving anything. I want you to trust me and TO DO what I'm going to tell you in just a minute."

A man of his word, Dave hesitated. If he said "Yes" - he knew that he would have no way out.

We both didn't know then how far and beyond it would take us. On my part, I was about to tell him something that was so common sense and even obvious to me, that I did it rather in passing.

"YES," - he said after a long pause, "I have nothing to lose. I'll do anything. Tell me."

"Dave, let me now tell you only the first step. Don't worry about the 2nd step. Don't worry about the 3rd step. Just record the next 10 consultations you do over the phone, white out the names, and send the audio files to me. We'll take it from there."

Dave relaxed. It was easy. His phone system recorded everything anyway. The vacation was over. He flew back to NY, and so did I.

What did I do when I received the recordings?

I went over the recordings quite a few times. Transcribed them all, combined them into one master text, broke into sections, conceptualized and summaried each section, as well as edited and polished them.

I came up with the final script and called up Dave.

"Dave, I know, the first step was easy, but I hope you know that you said YES to the whole thing, including all the steps, right?"

"What are you up to?"

"I am sending you back THE SCRIPT. Take a good guy, let the guy memorize the script, and test him. Make sure the guy is FLUENT and confident, make sure he knows the text like he knows his own name."

A few days later Dave calls me back, in shock and excitement - "I can't believe it! My guy brings to the office 5-6 prospects out of 10 callers! It's a different world!"

Let me pause here. It was a fascinating journey, and it would take quite a few hours to tell it over. But let's make a long story short and show the rest of the story to you from a bird's eye view.

The script was perfected. Not everybody was able to memorize it and say it over conversationally, interactively. But those who were - closed 7-8 out of 10.

The next step was an office consultation. It was much harder - as it was much longer, in comparison with a phone consultation. More material. More possibilities of branching out. But it was done too. Those who were able to memorize it and say it over interactively, in a conversation, became the star salespeople for the firm.

Dave tasted freedom and horizons expanded. But wait, it was only the beginning.

Please realize that ANY SUCCESS can (AND SHOULD) be captured. It can be captured as text, first transcribed, and then structured, polished and perfected.

Once ready, it can be used in MANY ways. As a script, as a pamphlet, as an audio, as a video, online, offline, as a sales letter, as an advertisement, as a basis for a seminar and a webinar, as a marketing device, as an educational tool, as a training tool for the employees, and so on - the sky and your imagination is the limit. It can be used to maintain and perfect the systems and processes in a business, AS WELL as a brilliant marketing solution when exposed to the potential clients or customers.

I don't want to oversimplify it. Of course there are details, subtleties, and technicalities. It takes a skill. But the heart of the matter is what copywriters call A COPY - the content, the captured, encapsulated SUCCESS. That is to say, if you are successful doing ANYTHING - capture EXACTLY what you are doing on a piece of paper - the captured content in a form of text is what we are calling A COPY in this context.

It changed Dave's life BIG TIME. And it can change YOURS. Well, the truth be told, his name is not Dave, but the story is true in all the details - including January, beach, Miami, and sunset.

It's applicable to ANY business, on ANY step of the process, on ALL stages of developing the relationship with clients or customers. Just capture - record, transcribe, analyze, structure, conceptualize, summarize, and express in A COPY - the text - this is what I call CAPTURED, ENCAPSULATED SUCCESS.

And then?

Well, BRAINSTORM the ways to use it - especially in marketing - there are many, many wonderful ways to use A COPY OF SUCCESS which can transform your business in many astonishing ways.

What IF I Give You $1,000,000 In Cash Today To Hire The Best Salespeople In The World?

Dear business owner,

You've been blessed with a wonderful business; you've been busy and successful.

However, you work hard, and you may wonder if you can grow your business further, or at the very least maintain the same level of success, without working even harder, without giving it even more of your precious time…

Let me ask you a question which will probably astonish you.

What IF I am giving you $1,000,000 - in cash? It's yours, you don't have to pay interest on it, and you don't have to pay anything back to me. But there is only ONE CONDITION: you have to spend this money to hire the best salespeople in the world.

Have you ever met them? Let me describe one of them.

This amazing salesperson doesn't think in terms of sales, but rather in terms of building your business. Your new hire listens more than speaks. Understands

DEEPLY your customers' and clients' needs, emotions, wants and doubts, their strengths and weaknesses. Knows your desires and aspirations and seeks to advance your cause in the world. Understands to the core your products and services, appreciates and shares your vision. Finds the best prospects and speaks to them from the heart. Fanatical about selling and works extremely intensely. Never accepts good enough as enough. Sees problems as opportunities and enjoys them immensely.

Of course I am not telling you news if I state that skillful and artful salesmanship is a powerful tool. It channels your products and services to the people, removes obstacles on the way, demonstrates and endears, resulting in sales, and sales, and sales. There is no greater blessing to any business than a great salesperson.

Where do you think you can take your business if this dream becomes a reality for you? Just imagine!

Well, that would be an ideal world, you may say, but where is the promised $1,000,000 in cash?

Here's the big news! THERE IS such a salesperson, and you DON'T need $1,000,000 in cash!

The name of a "salesperson" is a Sales Letter.

Defined as salesmanship in print and multiplied

salesmanship, a powerful sales letter is designed to sell your products and services to your bests prospects. It works as the best salesperson in the world, YET INFINITELY BETTER. Better - because it's multiplied, and ultimately much more impactful. But also, because it doesn't call in sick, doesn't have family issues, doesn't have moods, doesn't need to sleep, doesn't have any other interests in life, works 24/7, and after all performs at its best ALL the time!

A sales letter can change your business dramatically.

I prefer to use another term, commonly used by copywriters - A COPY - which is specifically referring to the content of a sales letter.

A COPY written by a GOOD copywriter may be easily worth $1,000,000 to you, and much more. Yet there is NO need to come up with $1,000,000 in cash. You can hire a professional copywriter for MUCH less than that, in a sense, INFINITELY less, in comparison with such a massive investment, and - what's even more important - in comparison with such a massive potential GAIN.

Let me explain you the concept of copywriting by means of a metaphor. Imagine hiring the best salesperson in the world BUT ONLY for a few weeks. You observe "magical" sales during this time, but... A few weeks are over and the salesperson leaves. But you've captured EVERYTHING the salesperson said to the prospects during the sales conversations, and you've transcribed it all, and now instead of talking to your prospects - you simply hand them a transcribed letter. You've captured the genius. You've encapsulated the brilliance. It's all in the letter now! Don't you think the letter will produce sales, and sales, and sales?

But this was a metaphor. Now let's get back to real life. Let me share with you what's happening behind the scenes. How is such a brilliant COPY (a.k.a. sales letter) created?

The truth is, it's not created. It's rather composed of the elements that ALREADY EXIST, the elements that YOU already HAVE. How so?

When we begin to work on your business, we meet with you. We shut down computers, phones, all other devices, and we talk. We talk for hours. What are we going to talk about?

About YOU, about your products, your services, your clients and customers, and… about much more. The depths and the layers will be unraveled. On a surface, you knew it all, yet you haven't heard and haven't seen it THIS WAY.

We record this conversation. After the meeting, I'll go over the recording over and over again. It's like digging and sifting to find golden nuggets.

Then I study your products and services. Deeply.

Then I study your clients, your customers, your prospects.

How do I study them? Well, it depends. You may have existing clients and customers, or you may be thinking of expanding to a new market, or you may be thinking of some prospects who have not come to you YET - whatever it is, with your help, I find a way to study THEM. In person or in forums, I am essentially going on a reconnaissance mission, at times pretty literally. I study them DEEPLY. Revealing the essence, the needs, the desires, the layers of meaning in their minds.

It's a fascinating process. We reveal, extract, capture, transform, connect, abstract, split, merge the "pieces" which are ALREADY there - in you, in your products and services, in your market - yet unnoticeable and unrecognizable until now. It's not so much creation, it's rather revelation and connectivity. Hence the power. Immense power. It's like unleashing the power of an atom - we don't create the power, it's there, it's been there all the time - yet NOBODY knew it until the time had come.

Step by step, A SALES COPY is born. Weaving A COPY from the subtle and definitive "particles" in you, in your vision, in your products and services, in your people, in your market. Crafting the SALES COPY which will transform your business and your life.

This is how YOUR SALES COPY is born, and this is why it works wonders. It sucks the reader in, takes the reader through in fascination, evokes an emotional response and motivates to buy, because it solves real problems, satisfies real desires, brings real solutions, and - most importantly - resonates with innermost thoughts and emotions.

Do you want to experience a power of COPYWRITING, an artful and skillful professionally crafted COPY which binds together you, your products and services, and your market?

P.S. The idea may seem unusual to you - why after all A COPY is a sort of a salesperson?!

Well, yes, and the idea is old. It was born well over a century ago, and the examples are plenty, perhaps many thousands, in every industry, in any time period.

Yet, the idea still hasn't caught up with many business owners, simply because A GOOD COPY takes SCIENCE, ART, TALENT, SKILL, and a HEART. It's a rare combination, isn't it?

Let's go back in time; I"ll show you a few concrete examples, and PLEASE keep in mind that the time does affect HOW you speak to your prospects, WHAT you are talking to them ABOUT, and WHO the prospects are. The time does not affect the essence of the phenomenon, just like the concept of a salesperson remains the same.

"Lift Up Your Eyes" COPY published by the Ford Motor Company had done more to popularize flying among the reading public than anything else before. It wasn't new - the planes were already flying, and people knew about it. Yet, it was this COPY that started the trend which would eventually make flying into the first choice of long distance transportation for the whole country.

You may be surprised to hear some commonly known brands as connected to the power of A COPY. For example, Listerine. Did you know that it was A COPY that sold Listerine to the whole country with such success that it became a winner almost overnight? The product was unknown and unpopular, but the legendary copy did its job. The "Often A Bridesmaid, But Never A Bride" COPY skyrocketed the sales and made the product so popular that Listerine remains at its high sales level until this day, many decades after the copy which brought it to life has been forgotten.

Another example. A young copywriter was assigned to sell the remaining 1,000 books called Encyclopedia of Etiquette. A masterful COPY was written and all the stock was sold almost overnight. But... most of the 1,000 books were returned. Why? Because the book itself was written before the turn of the century, and a few decades later the text and the pictures were ludicrously archaic. Would you call it a failure?

Wait, hear out the end of the story. The product was no

good, but THE COPY was a "salesperson" par excellence! Another, up to date version of the book was written, and... Using THE SAME BRILLIANT COPY that was composed for the outdated book, 2,000,000 copies of the newly written Book Of Etiquette were sold. Yes, two million! The brilliant salesperson - the COPY - did it swiftly.

You may wonder, if you write one piece of COPY, how long can it serve as a "salesperson"?

The legendary "Do You Make These Mistakes In English?" COPY sold one simple product to millions of people FOR OVER 40 YEARS! It was surely an exception, but A COPY that lasts years is a commonplace.

I chose the legendary examples from the first half of the last century. But the truth is that the examples are countless, especially today, when a choice of media is way beyond a printed sales letter or a newspaper article, and the trials can be done so quickly, easily, and cheaply in the age of Internet.

Would you like to have YOUR COPY in place? Would you like this faithful and brilliant "salesperson in print" to advance your sales, your business, your impact on the world?

How to slice your offer...
to generate more interest,
more prospects,
and ultimately more sales.

Let me demonstrate the offer slicing using an example.

Let's say you sell membership in a specialty gym, where you promote a certain type of exercise. Your offer is simple and makes sense: come to our gym, burn so much fat by means of this type of exercise.

Now let's slice it up. Focus on this specific type of exercise. Forget about the gym. Your offer is now partial, in comparison with the original offer: burn so much fat by means of this type of exercise.

If you put the offer this way, you would probably charge no money for it. But it doesn't mean it's free. Because people have to spend time and effort on this very exercise, and they have to give you at least their email in order for you to send them a few lessons about it. In this sense you still sell it - it's just that they pay with their time, effort, and email address - not with money.

Once they buy into the lesser offer, that is to say they are convinced that the exercise is worth their time and effort - at that point you can make a next offer: instead of doing this exercise home, where they don't have neither necessary equipment nor guidance and motivation - come to our gym to do this very type of exercise!

Realize that the original offer indeed contains two offers: one - activity, two - location. Sell activity alone first! Teach them this activity by itself, demonstrate it, explain its benefits, let them invest themselves into the activity. Only THEN take them to the next level by offering an "upgrade" to do the activity at the location.

If I buy into the activity - I'll definitely consider doing the activity in your location. But if I don't buy into the activity itself - I'll never consider doing it in the gym either.

Have you noticed how much stronger the sliced offer has become?

Instead of giving a one time offer and lose most of them - we slice it up, which helps us to establish the relationship with them first. We can now maintain the relationship, and make various offers as we go.

Learn to slice up your offers! Learn to notice how many offers your offers really contain! This will make quite a difference to your relationship with your prospects, and will surely multiply the sales manifold.

Will Your Copywriter Guarantee The Results?

Let's put it straight. Even the greatest of the greatest, legendary copywriters, almost miracle workers of marketing and sales, didn't hit the jackpot every single time. They had winners and they had losers. Their victories and failures alternated. Of course their winners were MANY, and their winners were BIG, yet NONE of them was able to create a winning copy every single time.

I don't know about you, but I find this fact fascinating. Just think about it. The legend - the greatest of the greatest, immensely skilled and experienced, getting paid fortune, having practically speaking unlimited resources and unlimited time, handling carefully researched handpicked projects - couldn't get it right every time? WHY NOT?

Truth be told, they indeed created a brilliant copy every single time, without exceptions. Yet a brilliant copy didn't work all the time. Because…

By the nature of the situation, I, as a copywriter, MUST accept certain assumptions you make as a business owner. I will surely try to minimize how many they are, and how big they are, yet my copy will inevitably be based on your assumptions to a certain extent.

If the assumptions are faulty - my copy won't succeed, even if it's a magical most brilliant copy ever written.

If the assumptions are right - my copy will be the winner.

Now back to the question I asked in the very beginning. Will your copywriter guarantee the results?

The answer is a definite no, and here is why.

Any business - always, without exceptions - implies taking a chance. If you win, you own your victory fully. If you lose, the failure is yours. It's the nature of investment.

Your business partners will share the risk with you. But your employees, your contractors, your clients and customers will NOT share the risk with you.

I, as a copywriter, do an excellent job. Sometimes - good and solid. Sometimes - brilliant and outstanding. I am a professional, and I guarantee my work - in the sense that I'll do a great job. But will I guarantee the results, the revenues, the ultimate success that the company seeks? Will I take a risk, sharing the investment risks with the owners? Will I take a chance, even if it's healthy and well justified, without becoming a full fledged business partner?

What's your answer?

Does a small business owner have to know the difference between Funnel Building and Copywriting?

What seems to be a game of words is in reality THE KEY for your business to succeed. The distinction between these 2 concepts is crucial, YET it's way too often completely overlooked.

If you don't mind, let me use my own terms. Nobody knows these terms besides you and me, so let me give you the definitions first.

"I can funnelize your business" means I can build a Funnel for your business.

"I can copytize your business" means I can create a great Copy, that is to say a great sales letter, that is to say a great persuasive and even selling text for your business.

Funnelizing VS. Copytizing!

So, let me ask you a question. Do you want me to funnelize your business OR copytize it?

The question is tricky, because…

First, if I build a funnel - of course I include the copy! How can I give you a funnel without a copy?! Pages with images and buttons with no text?!

Second, if I create a sales letter for your business - of course I imply a certain funnel, even if it's a simple one. After all any sales letter has a Call To Action which leads to the next funnel step, doesn't it? No sales letter can exist in vacuum, without an implied funnel. Okay, I as a copywriter wouldn't necessarily build the funnel, but at least I conceive it, and make the strategy and the steps clear. And if not - what kind of a sales letter is it?!

As you see, funnelizing includes copytizing, and copytizing contains the key elements of funnelizing.

The time has come to end the confusion.

As a funnel builder, I am working with YOU. My job is to extract from YOU the steps of the funnel, the target audience, the pains and attractions of the target audience. My direct involvement with your audience is minimal, if any. I assume that you know it all, and you know it right. I am dealing with YOUR mind, YOUR experience, YOUR vision.

On the contrary, as a copywriter, I am combining the three dimensions: 1) YOU (that is to say your knowledge, expertise, understanding), 2) your audience worldview (which often means a reconnaissance mission in some form - I have to immerse myself into your target audience, into their hearts and minds), and 3) my own creativity, revelations, understanding, insights.

It seems that copywriting is much more involved and effort-consuming, and in a sense it is true, BUT... The truth is that the relationship between copywriting and funnel building is NOT more/less, and is NOT better/worse. They are distinctly different, and you have to be very clear on the difference.

Funnel building makes much bigger assumptions about your vision of reality, about your vision of the target market, their needs and desires. There is a danger here: if you are OFF, the funnel will be OFF. And the life shows that way too often business owners are VERY OFF (this fact is counterintuitive, and as such is the subject on its own).

At the same time funnel building is focusing on the whole sales process, on designing and developing the multiple steps of the process, structuring the offer, optimizing and enriching the experience, creating the leverage - these are GREAT values, yet these values are conditioned by you being correct in your vision of the reality to begin with.

Copywriting hardly touches any of these. Even a powerful sales letter assumes a very simple process, the offer is usually taken as is, the experience is pretty simplistic.

YET copywriting connects with the reality more intimately, plugs into the target audience deeper, resonates more intensely, makes LESS assumptions about your vision of reality, and minimizes the remaining assumptions.

A word of warning: never combine the two. Don't funnelize and copytize at the same time. It will backfire. Pick one, whichever it is, and implement it fully. This will take you to an entirely new level. Then you may pick another one and proceed further, in case you're still not where you ultimately want to be.

So, equipped with the new understanding, do you want me to funnelize your business or copytize it? Your choice?

If I Am Your Copywriter, Which Of The 3 Fundamentally Different Approaches Do You Want Me To Employ?

The 1st approach.

I read an information kit you prepared for me about your products or services, and I am ready to proceed. By thinking creatively, by using my own imagination, I'm creating a copy. A sales letter is being created in the privacy of my own mind. I am interested in talking neither to you nor to your clients and customers. Little by little the copy is emerging.

Finally, a sales letter is ready. Happy and accomplished, I am handing it to you. Let's call this Creative Writing Copywriting.

The 2nd approach.

We meet with you in a comfy setting, over a cup of coffee, and we talk. For hours. I mostly ask questions. You do the talking. Don't be self-conscious about what you say. The more unconscious you are, the better. You are an expert, you are a professional, you are a visionary, BUT… For the most part, even you yourself are not aware of what's in your mind. Normally we deal with just a tip of an iceberg, leaving the rest underwater. This conversation's goal is to reach out far under the water, to empty out your mind, to visit and illuminate every dark corner.

After the conversation is over, I begin to work on a copy. I study the extensive notes I took. I also listen to the recording of the conversation again and again - to detect more meaning and more layers. Little by little the copy is emerging.

Finally, a sales letter is ready. Happy and accomplished, I am handing it to you. Let's call this Owner's Mind Copywriting.

The 3rd approach.

I am undertaking a reconnaissance mission. I am going into the midst of your prospects, and your clients and customers. I study them, I speak with them. Overtly and covertly, whatever is appropriate. I understand their pain points, their wants and desires, their hopes and goals. I am immersed in their world, I am accepting their worldview on myself. I now see the world through their eyes and hearts. I now see your products and services through their eyes and hearts.

When I am fully saturated with their lives, their problems, their worldview - I am coming back home. I begin to work on a copy. I am connecting their world with the world of your products and services. Little by little the copy is emerging.

Finally, a sales letter is ready. Happy and accomplished, I am handing it to you. Let's call this Their Worldview Copywriting.

Back to life. You're now familiar with the three fundamentally different approaches. I am your copywriter. Which of the approaches do you want me to employ for your business?

1. Creative Writing Copywriting (I am the source of the copy).
2. Owner's Mind Copywriting (you are the source of the copy).
3. Their Worldview Copywriting (your prospects, clients, customers are the source of the copy).

If you want to be politically correct, you'll probably choose the 3rd one. After all marketing is about them, not about us, isn't it?

If you have a great deal of self-confidence, you'll probably choose the 2nd one. After all you're an expert, and you indeed know it all, don't you?

If you're an idealistic dreamer, you'll probably choose the 1st one.

So, 1? 2? Or 3?

Would I surprise you if I say that ALL 3 have their well deserved place in the world of copywriting?

Let's understand the beauty and the power of each of the 3 approaches.

When would I employ creative writing as an engine behind my copy?

The answer is simple. When I myself belong to the target market. That is to say, I myself am a typical client or a customer for your products or services. A copy can be created simply by me speaking up, by expressing my own thoughts and emotions, by sharing my frustrations and victories.

When would I employ Owner's Mind Copywriting?

The answer is simple. Whenever the owner is available AND the owner LIVES through the clients' experiences, and is actually full of stories, ideas, feelings about the products and services, about prospects, clients, and customers. It still takes a great deal of work to extract a copy from the depths of the owner's mind, but at least it's all THERE, and thus can be done.

When would I employ Their Worldview Copywriting?

The answer is simple. Whenever I can reasonably easy get hold of potential and actual clients and customers, to penetrate their worldview, to understand their inner thoughts and emotions. Perhaps even to get in touch with them and to get their feedback.

Sometimes a winning copy originates from a skillful combination of all 3 approaches, but even then the main focus is on one of them.

Which one?

That's a million dollar question…

Funnels & You - Beyond The Obvious. Why & How A Funnel Can Transform Your Business.

There is a 2 minute explanation which is often employed to explain the funnels to beginner marketers. McDonald's is taken as an example.

It costs McDonald's $1.91 in advertising to get a customer into the drive thru. When they sell a burger for $2.09, the profit is 18 cents. Yet, when by means of a direction suggestion to a customer they upsell a coke and fries for $1.77 more, they keep $1.32 profit. The difference between $1.32 and 18 cents is impressive, especially considering that it was accomplished by adding just one more step into the sales process.

So, instead of a traditional 1-step sale you add a few more steps into the sales process. A few steps sales process becomes a funnel. A funnel maximizes your profits in comparison with more simplistic 1-step sales. After all in our example making a 2-step funnel increases the profit 8 times.

Simple?

Maybe. Yet brilliant and has brought millions in profits.

The step by step approach is the heart of the funnel method. Why is it so effective?

A prospect is gently guided through the funnel. In a traditional sale, the steps are either missing, or piled up together, or both. They are neither distinct nor connected in a progression. You can view a funnel sale as a guided expert sale, while a traditional sale is a non-guided sale.

Have you ever thought of having an expert, skilled and engaging Personal Shopper - online - FOR YOUR BUSINESS? Well, that's A FUNNEL!

Simple?

Maybe. Yet when you start thinking funnels, seeing funnels all over, and building funnels - your entire business experience is transformed.

Of course we focus on one funnel at a time. We design it, build it, fine-tune it. When it runs like clockwork, we may focus on another funnel. Over time your business will be represented by a harmonious system of intertwined funnels.

Funnels done right can transform ANY business TREMENDOUSLY. The process may include such elements as existing funnels analysis, competitors' funnels analysis, funnel strategy, restructuring the offer, funnel architecture, funnel design, funnel copywriting, and funnel building.

If you have a business - ANY business - there is a funnel that will work for you! A special funnel JUST FOR YOU.

So, what does a funnel mean to you?

It means EVERYTHING You Need To Market, Sell And Deliver YOUR Products Online! It means MORE leads, MORE clients, MORE customers, MORE sales!

Do you want more leads?

Let's talk common sense. There are three components you need to put together to accomplish the task.

1. A fresh new idea.
2. A resonating copy which is expounding the idea.
3. A funnel which embodies the copy.

This is the recipe, this is the prescription, there is nothing else that stands between you and multitudes of quality leads. The leads are just a funnel away from you!

When we work on the funnel, it's not just the funnel. The funnel by itself is only A BODY.

And what is the soul of the funnel?

The soul is a fresh new idea, and the great compelling and resonating COPY! We put all the ingredients together, and the funnel becomes ALIVE, ready to attract new leads, to excite them further, and to bring on new clients and customers...

Do you want more sales?
Do you want to sell your products & services online?

Let's talk common sense.

Assuming that your products and services are actually needed and wanted (otherwise you would be swimming against the powerful current), you need the two component to accomplish the task:

1. A sign which attracts your prospects' attention.
2. An expert guide, a personal shopper, a great sales consultant to take your prospects smoothly and gently through the sales process.

In fact, the presence of such a guide, and the quality of the guidance is exactly what makes the difference between your current sales and the desired much larger sales. The difference between a guided sale and a non-guided sale is HUGE.

So how do you do that?

One solution would be to hire the best salesperson you can find. Here you have an expert guide, a personal shopper, a sales consultant. The sales will skyrocket.

What's the problem though?

The problem is that you need to pay a huge salary, AND… One such a salesperson is most probably not enough for your business. Perhaps you need 10 or 100 or even 1,000 of them? Besides, we're looking for an online solution, aren't we?

So what's an online equivalent of an expert guide, a personal shopper, a great sales consultant?

A funnel! This is EXACTLY what the funnels are. This is the beauty and the power of funnels.

This is the recipe, and this is the prescription, there is nothing else that stands between you and so much more sales. Tons of sales are just a funnel away from you!

When we work on the funnel, it's not just the funnel. The funnel by itself is only A BODY.

And what is the soul of the funnel?

The soul is fresh ideas, unexpected angles, and the great compelling and resonating COPY based on your insight, your expertise, your knowledge and experience. We extract all the ingredients, and we put them all together. The funnel becomes ALIVE, ready to skyrocket your sales!

Do you want to take your business online?

I'm assuming you have an offline business. It works. It's successful.

You want to take it online. Why?

- Perhaps you want to scale it, and to skyrocket the sales?
- Perhaps you want to automate it - and make it so much easier to manage?
- Perhaps you want to reach out to so many more people, without having to go anywhere?
- Perhaps you want to build a better company image?
- Perhaps you want to make information more easily available to your clients and customers?
- Perhaps you want to lower operation and maintenance costs?
- Perhaps you want to acquire ability to do business 24/7?
- Perhaps you're attracted to low start up costs?
- Perhaps you want you business to no longer depend on a physical location?
- Perhaps you want a global reach?
- Perhaps you're looking for new opportunities for growth?

Whatever your reasons are, I have a suggestion for you. It's a good suggestion. You'll surely appreciate it. It works in the vast majority of situations, and I hope it will work for you.

Taking a business online is not a small matter. It may take time and investment. It may not go smoothly, after all you've never done it before, have you?

However, let's not rush to take your ENTIRE business online. That will happen when the time comes. Let's take your LEAD GENERATION online - ONLY the lead generation, for the time being.

You can surely see a few reasons WHY this is a good idea, so I won't bother listing them. However, let me tell you the BIGGEST reason why this is much more than just a good idea.

The most difficult, the most challenging, the most unpredictable element of the online business is lead generation. In a sense, everything else is a matter of putting together technicalities and technologies, as well as taking care of a few details. Everything else is DOABLE, while the lead generation is either doable OR NOT. If it goes wrong - everything else is simply dead, regardless of how brilliant it is and how much effort, time, and money have gone into building it.

When you figure out how to bring the leads - the rest of the business can be built online in stages. It just becomes clear what has to be done and how. In fact, who and what the leads are, and HOW EXACTLY they come to you online - usually determines the structure and the angles for the rest of the business.

So how do you generate leads online?

You need the two component to accomplish the task:

1. A sign which attracts your prospects' attention.
2. An expert guide, a personal shopper, a great sales consultant to take your prospects smoothly and gently through the process.

The presence of such a guide, and the quality of the guidance is exactly what makes the difference between few disinterested leads and multitudes of excited leads eager to know more from you, more about you (or your products and services). The difference between guided experience and non-guided experience is HUGE.

And what's an online equivalent of an expert guide, a personal shopper, a great sales consultant?

A funnel! This is EXACTLY what the funnels are. This is the beauty and the power of funnels.

The multitudes of leads are just a funnel away from you!

When we work on the funnel, it's not just the funnel. The funnel by itself is only A BODY.

And what is the soul of the funnel?

The soul is fresh ideas, unexpected angles, and the great compelling and resonating COPY based on your insight, your expertise, your knowledge and experience. We extract all the ingredients, and we put them all together. The funnel becomes ALIVE, ready to bring you leads, and lead, and leads.

When the stream of the fresh and eager leads is established, and you are comfortable, feeling in control, you can now build more funnels to establish your presence online, one stage at a time. You will surely succeed!